THE S...

OF
HAPPINESS

100 Ways to True Fulfilment

Ben Renshaw

Vermilion
LONDON

1 3 5 7 9 10 8 6 4 2

First published in 2003 by Vermilion,
an imprint of Ebury Press, Random House,
20 Vauxhall Bridge Road, London SW1V 2SA

Random House Australia (Pty) Limited
20 Alfred Street, Milsons Point, Sydney, New South Wales
2061, Australia

Random House New Zealand Limited
18 Poland Road, Glenfield, Auckland 10, New Zealand

Random House South Africa (Pty) Limited
Endulini, 5A Jubilee Road, Parktown 2193, South Africa

The Random House Group Limited Reg. No. 954009

Papers used by Vermilion are natural, recyclable products
made from wood grown in sustainable forests

Printed and bound by Nørhaven Paperback A/S, Denmark

A CIP catalogue record for this book
is available from the British Library

ISBN 00-9188754-2

I dedicate this book to my daughter India,

who is the symbol of happiness in my life.

Acknowledgements

Gratitude is the gateway to happiness. Thank you to my wife Veronica for her amazing love, friendship and fun. Thank you to Robert Holden for being a never-ending source of wisdom, inspiration and friendship. Thank you to David White for making the difference with this book, I treasure your support and friendship. Thank you to my family for always believing in me. Thank you to everyone at The Happiness Project for your pioneering spirit. Thank you to my editor Judith Kendra for your encouragement.

Introduction

What is your idea of happiness? Is it lying on a Mediterranean beach? Is it financial freedom? Is it a new pair of shoes? Is it getting stuck into the garden on a Sunday afternoon? Or, like mine, winning a game of tennis? Whatever it is, you know that feeling won't last forever – but what if there is another way? What if it could go on and on?

This book explores what real happiness is. It uncovers the blocks that may have prevented us from fully experiencing it and gives timely reminders for keeping us on track. It is based

on our work at The Happiness Project, a
unique enterprise offering courses in
happiness, success and relationships.

In this fast-changing and unpredictable world,
it's a wise move to unravel happiness. Choose
it, feel it, know it, hold it, breathe it, play with
it – that's what this book is about. Ultimately, it
will enable you to give up the pursuit of
happiness and come home to a place of peace
and true fulfilment.

1

You are already happy!

Picture the sunshine – always shinning, radiant, warm and inviting. The trouble is that we don't always see it.

This is true of our innate happiness. It already exists within us – it is always present and available.

We are born happy. It is in our DNA. We instinctively know what it is. We don't have to figure it out.

Then life's turbulence arrives, bringing with it conflict, pain, anguish and heartbreak. As we experience these storms we can get disconnected from our happiness. It can get cut off, becoming a forgotten memory. Sometimes it requires a wake-up call for us to remember.

This book is about reconnecting you to what is already yours – happiness.

Be prepared for new beginnings.

2

Choose
happiness

Cast your mind back to your morning
performance upon awakening today. Was it a
beautiful performance? Did you rise and shine,
or rise and whine? Did you greet the day with
'Good Morning, God' or 'Good God!
Morning'? In particular, what choices did you
make in your first waking moments? When I
ask most people this question the responses
include things such as: 'Hit the snooze button',
'Tea or coffee?', 'What to wear?', 'Feed the

dog'. It's inspirational stuff. Then I ask if they have consciously chosen to be happy. It is a rare occurrence.

It is easy to forget that happiness is a choice we can make. Just as much as we choose our wardrobe, we can also choose our approach to life. Choosing happiness is like pushing an intention button. A powerful intention, which once deployed will reap great joy.

Don't miss another moment. Upon awakening tomorrow choose happiness and watch it inspire your day.

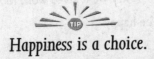

Happiness is a choice.

3

Happiness is...free

What have you told yourself you have to do in order to earn happiness? How much do you think you have to work? How many hours do you have to put in? How much overtime do you believe is required?

Many of us have been brought up on messages that you have to earn happiness, for example 'There is no such thing as a free lunch'. We are suspicious. We tell ourselves there must be a catch. As a result we tend to work too hard in order to be happy.

Consider the possibility that happiness does not have to be earned. That it's free.

It is inherent within you.

Let this idea help you to remove any blocks that you may be holding on to. Say to yourself, 'A block I have to happiness is…' and listen to your answer. Your willingness to release blocks sets you free.

Happiness is free.
You don't have to earn it.

4

Happiness is...a state of mind

A very successful self-made businesswoman came to see me suffering from frustration and unhappiness. She had a wonderful house, a dream kid and a lifestyle to match. She admitted that something was missing – happiness.

We all have a story about happiness and how it has eluded us. And to be quite honest nobody is exempt, not even the wealthy, the beautiful or the famous. The trouble is we've been looking in the wrong places.

Happiness is not a tangible thing; it is a state of mind. Learn to develop a state of mind conducive to happiness. Imagine yourself free of worries, limitations and distractions. Picture your mind like a placid lake. Decide to let go of your troubled thinking and watch happiness bubble up from within.

Stop looking for happiness
in the wrong places.

5

Happiness is a natural state

Having spent my childhood immersed in violin practice, I decided, after much soul-searching, that the music profession was not for me. I realised that what really grabbed me was people, their problems and finding ultimate solutions.

I began learning psychology and the study of problems. I learnt about pain, struggle, conflict, helplessness, addiction, suffering and advanced suffering. I became an expert problem-spotter. Although I loved problems, what I came to realise was everybody wanted to be happy, whatever it meant to them. I also recognised that once problems were resolved, happiness would emerge quite spontaneously.

Since those early days I have reappraised my problem orientated approach and have come to see that happiness is a natural condition that doesn't require treatment. Now when clients come to me, instead of looking for their problems, I focus on their underlying happiness and allow that to inspire their growth and healing.

If you're happy, it's OK.

6

Happiness is your eternal partner

Do you suffer from commitment phobia? Do you find yourself wanting to run at the first hurdle in a relationship? Do you feel trapped and suffocated by your partner?

If so, now is your opportunity to heal. Imagine a relationship in which all your needs are met, no strings attached. Picture yourself surrounded by all the space and support you require. Sounds good? This is what happiness offers you and more – the only requirement is that you let yourself receive it.

I love the idea that happiness is yours forever. It will never let you down, reject or abandon you. This is because happiness is available 24/7. When people say that they cannot find happiness, or that it seems to have deserted them, the fact is that their awareness of happiness has temporarily disappeared. By recognising that happiness is your eternal partner you attune yourself to it each day.

Take happiness down the aisle.

7

Happiness is selfless

Another traffic jam. You're late. Somebody is indicating to pull into your lane ahead of you. Are you filled with a sense of friendly compassion? Do you let them in with a big smile? I doubt it!

Unfortunately, stressful circumstances make us selfish. We become withdrawn and even antagonistic. We have less to give, and when we do give, our giving is often conditional.

On the other hand, when you're happy you naturally want to give without conditions. You'll let the driver in ahead of you without even expecting a wave in return.

One of the most unhelpful beliefs about happiness is that it's selfish. Nothing could be further from the truth. Happy people are more open and willing to reach out and help others.

Let your happiness inspire you to give.

Happiness is...
a way of seeing

John was in a difficult life situation. He was a full-time carer looking after his elderly father, and his view of life had become tainted. In our work together it became clear that he needed to change the way he perceived his situation.

He agreed to see that there were gifts he could give and receive each day, and this helped him to develop a greater acceptance of his caring role.

We cannot always change the circumstances of our lives. We may not want to. What we can do is change the way we see our life in order to bring about a fresh perspective. Ask yourself, 'How could I see my life differently?' and let inspiration carry you forward.

Shift your perception
to transform your life.

9

Believe in happiness

Do you believe that happiness is an impossible dream? Do you believe that it's always followed by a fall? If so, it's not surprising if happiness seems to elude you. Your beliefs are self-fulfilling. Change them and you change your reality.

Ask yourself, 'What does it cost me to not believe in happiness?' Could the price be too high? A lack of joy, a lack of fulfilment and a lack of trust?

Now focus on how you can benefit by believing in happiness again. Believing in happiness is a great confidence booster. It plants a seed of possibility which you can nurture until you're filled with a glorious certainty.

You'll *see* happiness
when you *believe* in it.

10

Size does matter

When you're a tourist faced with something grand like the Eiffel Tower, the Golden Gate Bridge or the Taj Mahal, it's easy to lose yourself in the enormity of the spectacle and forget the importance of the details that have gone into its making.

This is true of life itself. We can become overwhelmed by the apparent magnitude of it all and ignore the extraordinary detail that goes into its creation.

It's time to refocus your binoculars on the small details that occur each moment and which if valued add up to make life worth living.

When I ask people what makes them happy, they talk about little things such as a smile, a kind gesture, a bunch of flowers or somebody just saying thank you.

Once you adopt this attitude you will recognise that each moment is filled with a potential gift.

Enjoy the little details of today.

11

Happiness is... unreasonable

Are you happy? No, I've got too many things to do.

Are you happy? No, I haven't got enough money in the bank.

Are you happy? No, I haven't got a partner.

The list goes on.

Imagine being happy despite the above. This is real happiness. It recognises our difficulties but doesn't bend to them. It embraces them with acceptance and compassion but doesn't lose its own sense of self.

At The Happiness Project we prescribe 'unreasonable happiness'. This is a happiness that transcends the everyday problems we all experience. Ask yourself, 'Am I ready to be unreasonably happy?' Notice any resistance that you may have to this idea and smile.

Make a list of the things that
you 'need' in order to be happy,
and throw it away.

12

Give thanks

What do you experience when you are happy?
The majority of people talk about feeling
immense gratitude for family and friends, true
appreciation for the little things in life and
heartfelt thanks for the multitude of gifts that
they receive every day. There is no doubt that
gratitude and happiness go hand in hand.

Giving thanks is not a technique to make you happy. It is a reflection of valuing life. Practise now. Think about three things that you are grateful for. Start small. For instance, maybe you are thankful for waking up in the morning. Perhaps you are grateful for a work opportunity, or for having a particular friend in your life.

As you give thanks you will find more things to be thankful about.

Make gratitude your attitude for life.

13

Pleasure passes

We have our wires crossed. For so long our society has had happiness mixed up with pleasure. We've become adrenaline junkies seeking the next pleasure high that will give us a hit. Whether it's making tons of money, extensive retail therapy, exotic holidays, delicious chocolate, fine wine or love-making, the pleasure we seek cannot be sustained.

This is because the nature of pleasure is transitory and is specifically connected to our senses. Conversely, the nature of happiness is connected to our spirit.

No amount of pleasure can yield real happiness, as the two are different worlds. There is nothing wrong with pleasure – it is pleasurable; but don't expect happiness to extend directly from it.

Enjoy pleasure but don't bank
your happiness on it.

14

Unhappiness is OK

One of the main questions I'm asked as co-director of The Happiness Project is 'Are you always happy?' For the record, no! I certainly experience unhappiness. However, I have learnt that once you make peace with unhappiness, it is no longer a problem. Unhappiness is a message. It is telling us something. When I listen to my unhappiness it is usually telling me things such as slow down, rest up and get back into balance.

The next time you experience unhappiness ask yourself, 'What is this unhappiness telling me? What can I learn from it?' Receive the gift it offers and move on. Remember that real happiness is not the absence of unhappiness; it is the capacity to be kind to yourself whatever you are feeling.

Unhappiness has something to tell us.
Listen.

15

Age is no barrier

When I was twelve, I thought that the teenage years would be the best of my life. By the age of sixteen it became clear to me that it had to be in my twenties. By my mid-twenties I was rapidly consoling myself that it could only get better in my thirties. I'm still waiting!

The time has come to stop using age as a reason for happiness.

There is no optimum age to be happy. Growing older may bring about a different perspective on life, but it doesn't guarantee anyone happiness.

If you have been waiting for a specific time in order to be happy, re-evaluate now.

Don't hold off. Now is the best age for happiness.

16

Embrace
the past

When I entered the world of personal
development I spent a considerable amount of
money trying to get rid of my past. I attended
many courses, read many books and went to
many therapists in order to break its hold on
me. This proved impossible. In fact I gradually
realised that the way to heal my past was to
accept it rather than to reject it.

Where are you still unresolved with your past? What areas still cause you pain? What relationships are involved? Imagine extending acceptance to these areas and making peace with them. By burying the hatchet and stripping off the suit of armour you've been wearing you will find that life is lighter and happiness is present.

See your past as your friend.

17

Now is the point

I am often asked, 'When does happiness happen?' The answer is now, now and now. One of the great spiritual truths is that everything you desire is wrapped up in the present moment. The trouble is that we spend most of our time caught up in the past or focused on the future and therefore we miss out on happiness now.

Use this opportunity to focus on the present moment fully. Close your eyes, take a deep breath and experience this moment. Notice the temptation for your mind to wander. Gently bring it back to now. How do you feel?
Commit to living in the now in order to give happiness its greatest chance.

When you look at your watch,
remind yourself that the real time
is now.

18

Make way for happiness

Have you ever found yourself trying to think of someone's name or an answer to a question and drawn a blank? The more you force it the less able you are to remember. Probably, five minutes later, when you're doing something completely different, up it pops.

This is how happiness happens. Get your questioning, logical mind out of the way and happiness shows up.

The trouble is that we have been trained to use rational thinking and we've become good at it. Psychologists estimate that we think up to 40,000 thoughts per day. But you can't think your way to happiness.

You need to set aside a space for happiness. This requires you to empty your mind of all the clutter. If you already meditate, good move. If you don't, it may be a good idea to take five minutes out each day to sit, do nothing and simply let happiness in.

Space and stillness are great for happiness.

19

Happiness is...not a carrot

We live in a world of advertising. Every day
we are bombarded with hundreds of messages
tempting us to part with our time, energy and
attention. But are we clear about what we are
focusing on?

Carrots are goals that we dangle in front of
ourselves. Our belief system tells us that we

won't be happy until we've achieved them.
For instance, a carrot may be the next position
at work, more money or a new wardrobe.
However, this way of thinking just serves to
delay happiness continually.

It's great to have goals but remember that their
value lies in the process of their achievement,
not the final outcome.

Ask yourself, 'What do I want?' Ask yourself,
'What do I really want?' Keep on doing this
until you reach your bottom line truth.

Eat a carrot once a day as a reminder
that happiness is available to you now.

Happiness is… deep and meaningful

Maybe happiness appears to you as frivolous and superficial, but in fact real happiness has a depth that goes to the core of your being. The stereotyped image of a happy clappy person could not be further from the truth.

Coming to understand happiness forces you to ask big questions in life such as 'Who am I?', 'What is my purpose?' and 'What do I want to give?'

Being happy connects you to an authenticity that takes you beyond the surface of everyday life. It enables you to celebrate what is most meaningful for you.

Ask yourself, 'What is real and true for me?' and put it at the centre of your existence.

Live your truth in order to be happy.

Happiness is contagious – catch it!

Are you willing to take a challenge and play a game? With each of the next five people you meet I'd like you to share a different piece of good news. That's right, one person equals one piece of happiness. Make a note of what happens.

This game is one of our favourite exercises at
The Happiness Project. It is remarkable the
responses you hear from people. Blank faces
turn into sparkling eyes and large smiles as
people begin to talk about and listen to happy
stories.

It's so common to play life down rather than
celebrate it.

Cook a delicious meal, help a friend out or
make a child laugh. These are powerful
reminders of how great happiness is.

*Make a deal with yourself
to share happiness with others.*

22

Welcome happiness in

You have prepared a delicious dinner. Candles are burning, music is playing and you're waiting for your guest to arrive. There is a knock on the door. As you open it a wonderful light enters the room. Welcome happiness!

Imagine inviting happiness into your world just as you would a great friend. Every time you take a step towards happiness, it will take two more towards you. It's a wonderful dance.

The truth about happiness is that it is a great companion and you need to treat it as one.

By extending your hospitality you will let happiness have a permanent place in your home.

Invite happiness into your life each day.

23

Be spontaneously available

Christmas day is looming and the pressure to be happy is mounting. As the family gather, everyone puts on a brave face. Tension is audible and painted smiles are cracking. Sometimes it's on those occasions when we're supposed to be most happy that we're most miserable.

You can't plan happiness because trying to deliver it on a plate squashes creativity, fun and joy.

What if you approached this scenario from a different angle?

Let go of the preparation. Allow yourself to be spontaneously available rather than using force or sheer effort. Being spontaneously available is about letting go of preconceived expectations, then being fully present, ready and open to happiness.

*When you think you know
what's going to happen, pause.
Let yourself be spontaneously available.*

24

Make happiness a priority

It's only too easy for happiness to slide down our list of priorities. As the demands of family, work and home take over, we tend to lose it in the everyday hubbub. We can believe that it is not as important as everything on our 'to do' list. As a consequence it becomes a distant memory.

Learn to prioritise happiness.

Don't wait until you've cleared your inbox and
completed your chores. There will always be
something in the way. Decide to make
happiness come first. Wear it like a badge.
Shine it and make it as colourful as possible.
Your commitment to happiness will add a new
dimension to your family, your work and
your life.

Dare to make happiness a priority.

25

Travel light

Since life is a journey, you can decide how you want to travel along the way. Be it first class or economy, it is up to you how you enjoy the ride.

The choice to travel light means letting go of any baggage – fears, grievances and pain that hold you down and prevent you from flying. The key to a sustained flight is your willingness to let go.

Ask yourself, 'What do I need to let go of in order to fly at such a high altitude?' For instance, if guilt is weighing you down, commit to forgiving yourself and reclaiming your natural innocence. If fear is playing havoc with your perceptions, recognise that you're probably caught in the past and it's time to move on.

Since we are all just passing through on this journey, your decision to wear the world as a loose garment will carry you along gracefully.

The more you let go, the higher you'll fly.

26

Money is not the answer

I once appeared on a television show about
whether money can make you happy. On the
show with me were lottery winners, self-made
millionaires, those with inherited wealth and
those who had lost fortunes. No matter what
each of our backgrounds, though, the overall
conclusion we all formed was that money can
rent you happiness, but it can't buy it.

If it were a fact that money equalled happiness then every wealthy person would be happy. We know that not to be the truth.

Money can help – of course it can. At least you can arrive at your problems in style!

Start by asking yourself, 'What will money bring me?' Is it greater security, peace of mind, freedom? Whatever it is, commit to those attributes right now, without necessarily having the bank balance to match.

It's not money, it's your attitude to money that makes the difference.

27

Give up
the search

Have you heard the story about the laughing
Buddha? The one about the man who grew up
a prince, renounced his title and went out into
the world in search of truth. After having lived
years of rigorous asceticism and then given it
up, he finally woke from a night's sleep to
realise that he had attained enlightenment! In
this moment the Buddha laughed out loud as

he came to see that what he had searched for already existed within him.

This is the great cosmic joke.

You are what you seek! The happiness, joy, peace and inspiration that you look for live within you. Turn your gaze around. Give up the search. Come home to yourself and realise that happiness is within.

**Every day remind yourself
that you are what you seek.**

28

There are no rules

Do you feel boxed in? Do you have no room to breathe? Does it seem as if you have created a set of rules in order to be happy?

If so, according to Dr Albert Ellis, the founder of Rational Emotive Therapy, you're suffering from a condition he calls 'Musterbation'.

'I must tick off my to do list', 'I must be nice to everyone all the time', 'I must not get angry', 'I must keep my house tidy', 'I must answer the phone after two rings'. No wonder you feel trapped in a box.

These 'musts', 'oughts' and 'shoulds' infiltrate our lives. The truth is that we may want to fulfil some of these behaviours, but once they become rules our natural desire disappears and they turn into a heavy burden.

Ask yourself, 'What must happen in order for me to be happy?' Then remove the 'must' and see if it still appeals.

Turn your rules into choices.

29

Happiness is... not a deserving matter

Having a baby daughter means that I get out of the house more, as I walk her around the local park. On one occasion, noticing a feeling of tension in my stomach and not knowing its cause, I decided to listen to what the tension was telling me. It was a beautiful summer's morning, and by rights I should have been feeling perfectly happy, but a voice I have come to know so well was getting in the way.

'You don't deserve to be happy. You haven't done enough to deserve it. You haven't worked hard enough, achieved enough or contributed enough.'

I had to smile, because I would never tell my daughter, India, that she couldn't be happy because she didn't deserve it!

Believing that you have to deserve happiness comes about through a feeling of unworthiness. Learn to accept that happiness is your birthright and that you don't have to do anything to deserve it.

Be open to undeserved happiness.

30

Be optimistic

As a new father I've made it part of my research to look for cynical babies – I've yet to find one! I believe that we enter this world as optimists and that cynicism is a learned behaviour resulting from the way that we interpret our life experiences.

But let me ask you this: who is right, the cynic or the optimist? They both are, it depends on how you see things. The choice is yours. However, there is clearly a strong link between optimism and happiness.

This was confirmed to me when I recently worked with Boots on their Wellbeing 2002 project. The research was set up to identify the main factors that contribute to our sense of wellbeing. I was gratified to see that optimism came very high up on the list. A person's willingness to see opportunity in any given situation contributed to their feeling of wellbeing and ultimately happiness.

Ask yourself, 'How can I see more opportunity in my life?' Then seize it!

Look for the silver lining in every problem.

31

Sign a willingness contract

Have you ever found yourself holding on to one particular point of view? Stubbornly resisting new ideas, new horizons and a fresh perspective? Unable to bend in the face of change? Will you do anything rather than accept another viewpoint?

Would you be willing to give up this resistance? If not, would you be willing to be willing?

In my work with clients I often find that we need to take willingness to extremes. It is at the very heart of making progress yet it can become blocked by fear.

The first step in the happiness journey is simply to be willing. This means that you open yourself to new possibilities rather than holding on to your old inflexible self.

Ask yourself on a scale of 0–10 how willing you are to be happy. With every passing day imagine yourself going up a notch. This will keep you open to happiness.

Your willingness starts
with a change of heart.

32

Entertain possibility thinking

When I first studied the power of the mind, positive thinking was very popular. Although developing a positive mindset is important, I found that when I was unhappy the most unhelpful thing anybody could tell me was, 'Think positive'. It appeared so false and far from where I was at the time that it only made things worse.

Then I came across the idea of possibility thinking. Possibility thinking is being willing to consider another way of thinking. For instance, if you are feeling unhappy ask yourself, 'What possibilities can I think of right now?' You could consider the possibility that unhappiness is telling you something you need to hear – that there is a valuable lesson to learn.

The gift of possibility thinking is that it opens new doors and creates new horizons.

Become a 'possibility thinker'.

33

Now is new

Stuck in a rut? Can't get out? You probably didn't plan to get into it, but you're there anyway. It is very unlikely that you awoke one morning and said, 'Today I'm going to get into a rut!'

The truth is we can find ourselves in a rut without even knowing how it happened. Relax. Help is at hand.

Recognise that within each moment is a new beginning. This provides the opportunity to see things differently and to act on them. It sounds simple but it works.

All you need to do is see life afresh.

Drop your cynicism. Let go of your grievances and commit to a new beginning. Why? Because the gifts you will receive are priceless.

**Every moment
has something new to offer.**

34

Forgive first

Kim had enough reasons to be unhappy forever. Married to a violent, deceitful man, her unhappiness had been compounded by years of abuse. Eventually her divorce was finalised. She won custody of the children and moved back to her home country, but still she felt unresolved and in pain.

Although she had broken free from her unhappy circumstances, it was only when Kim and I worked together to help her forgive herself and ultimately her ex-husband that a sense of a new happiness began to emerge.

If you have been looking for a way to heal grievances, upsets and heartbreak, then look no further.

Forgiveness is your answer.

It is the catalyst for change. The key to forgiveness is your willingness. Let forgiveness forgive for you. It has the wisdom to alleviate your suffering and return you to love.

Forgiveness is the decision to focus on love and let go of the rest.

35

Forgive
yourself

Can you see that the amount of grievance you
hold against yourself equals the amount of
unhappiness you experience? Stored
grievances in the form of self-judgement, self-
attack and damaging self-beliefs are heavy
weights to carry.

The first step to undo these types of grievance
is to forgive yourself. Self-forgiveness is the
willingness to see yourself differently.

Where you judge yourself, extend kindness.
Where you attack yourself, lay down your
arms.

Forgiving yourself is not a technique; it is a
philosophy. Forgiving yourself is not
something you do once; it is a way of life.
Remind yourself that you are not your
thoughts or your actions. Who you really are is
a spiritual presence that you reconnect with
every time you choose to forgive yourself.

Make forgiveness a way of life.

36

Forgive others

'He/she is impossible.' 'He/she never listens to me.' 'He/she just wants to ruin my life.' Who are you still attacking? Who do you still judge negatively? Who do you still hold grievances against? Be brutally honest as you ask yourself these questions because the extent to which you are willing to forgive others mirrors the extent to which you are willing to be happy.

The art of forgiving others involves recognising the distinction between their essence and their behaviour. Naturally if you have suffered some form of abuse I'm not suggesting that you should endorse the abuser's actions. You can forgive someone and condemn their behaviour. In fact through forgiving someone you are able to understand their actions. This will then enable you to heal any pain or wound and will set you free to live your life fully.

Whenever you are tempted to attack, first decide to forgive.

37

Be a bit kinder

At a conference I gave for social workers working with people with cancer, one lady made a comment that really stood out. She noted that the patients she worked with, who were nearing the end of their lives, found that what made the difference in coping with their pain and distress was the level of kindness that they received.

An act of genuine kindness helps to wash away troubled thoughts. It gives rise to greater clarity and peace of mind and enables someone to feel loved and appreciated

.

Don't wait to give the gift of loving kindness. As you extend it to others your life will be touched in ways that you cannot even comprehend. Kindness goes straight to the heart of the matter.

Commit to an act of kindness daily.

38

Feelings need feeling

When I entered the world of personal development one of my major goals was to rid myself of feelings. I was wracked by feelings of angst, fear and tension. I naively believed that if I had no feelings, I could be happy – wrong!

We're human. Feelings are an essential part of our make-up. If we don't honour them we run into trouble. All that a feeling ever needs is to be felt.

The trouble is that we get nervous about feelings. It's time to change the trend.

Learn to make peace with your difficult feelings by accepting them. As you extend acceptance you will find that they no longer have the power they once held. In fact you will discover that there is a gift that lies within each feeling.

Practise accepting your feelings
in order to receive their inherent gifts.

39

You are not your feelings

We may have feelings but they do not define who we are. Sometimes it is difficult to remember this. I think back to a client named Clare who suffered from clinical depression. When originally diagnosed by her psychiatrist, she was told that there was something wrong with her. In Clare's darkest moments she merged with her feelings and believed that she was her illness. She had lost her true identity.

Our work together involved the delicate process of undoing this perception and disentangling Clare's two worlds. Ultimately, she was able to stand back and recognise that she was not her feelings. She had the experience of depression but it was not her true self. Say to yourself; 'I am unhappy.' Then say, 'I am experiencing unhappiness.' What differences did you notice? Become aware of the space between yourself and the feeling. This allows you to recognise that you are not your feelings.

We have feelings but they do not define our true selves.

Be aware of not merging your identity with your feelings.

40

Fear is behind you

'I want a relationship but I'm afraid of rejection.' 'I want to go for a job interview but I'm afraid of failure.' 'I want to travel but I'm afraid of the unknown.' We are all familiar with this voice. I call it the voice of fear. But it could also be called the voice of the past.

I believe that fear is the outcome of our perceptions, and our perceptions are governed by our past. For instance, if you were rejected in a previous relationship or job, the probability is that your confidence will be eroded now.

It's time to close the door on letting the past dominate your present. See F.E.A.R as False Evidence Appearing Real, and recognise that your past perceptions are always fallible.

Whenever you are in fear,
ask yourself, 'Is this fear real,
or is it just a fear?'

41

Get off the worry cycle

Do you love to worry? Would you describe yourself as a professional worrier? Do you catch yourself worrying because you're not worrying?

Be honest with yourself for a moment: how much anxiety does it take to solve a problem? None. Anxiety does not give rise to a solution.

But the professional worrier believes that as long as they worry then everything will be OK. Worry is a futile attempt to feel in control. It wastes vast amounts of time and energy as well as destroying your peace of mind. In truth you have only a certain amount of control. Therefore if you cannot influence something directly, let it go and move on.

*Write down your worries
and then let them go.*

42

Even this will pass

Have you ever had an argument with your partner? Felt lousy and thought that the relationship was doomed? How long did these feelings last?

It's ironic that when we're feeling bad we think it will last forever, and yet when we're happy we know only too well that it will pass!

The trouble with unhappiness is that it manages to collapse our perspective, leaving us feeling as if we have no room to breathe.

We forget that the one guarantee in life is that change is inevitable. Everything passes, even misery. Remember this the next time you're feeling stressed and challenged. It will make a difference.

At difficult moments tell yourself, 'Even this will pass.'

43

Don't edit yourself out

Are you aware of an inner voice that tells you to keep quiet, not to contribute your ideas or stories because anything you say isn't worthwhile? Welcome to the 'editor' of your life. Familiar tactics of the 'editor' include:

- Preventing us from giving our input at meetings.
- Stopping us sharing our stories at dinner parties.
- Inhibiting us from showing a sense of humour.
- Blocking us from doing the work of our dreams.

- Telling us that we shouldn't be thinking above our station.
- Ridiculing our sense of self-worth.

The trouble is that the 'editor' erases everything about us. When we edit ourselves out of our lives, what's left? A shadow. We are literally wiped out. If we're not here, then happiness isn't here either. Decide now to override the 'editor' in order to let yourself be seen fully for who you really are.

Allow yourself to be everything that the 'editor' tries to block.

44

Stop trying

Put this book down for a moment. Now try to pick it up. Don't just pick it up, try to pick it up. What happened? How did it feel? What did you think? Now pick it up. Once again notice your response. What was different? Did you find that not trying to pick it up made it easy and effortless?

Trying to be happy is not a recipe for happiness. It involves excessive effort and confused thinking that removes us from our natural state. We tend to slip into a trying mode when we are unsure of how to do something. We falsely believe that more effort will bring us the results we so desire. This is particularly frustrating when applied to happiness because the more we try to be happy the more elusive happiness becomes.

Ask yourself, 'How can I try less and be more happy?' Follow the answer you receive.

Trying is an indication that you're not trusting.

45

End struggle

I was addicted to struggle. If something was easy it had no appeal. My wife Veronica was the opposite. If something was a struggle she had no interest. We clashed! I was convinced that struggle was a necessity for happiness. She trusted that good things would just happen. I struggled with her philosophy – until I kept seeing her easily fulfilled. This helped me to change my mind.

Ask yourself, 'How much struggle does it take for me to be happy? How many financial worries, relationship dramas, work crises and health problems do I need?' If you score high on the 'compulsive need to struggle' list, stop now. It can seriously damage your happiness.

We have our wires crossed. Happiness doesn't require struggle. It comes about through letting go and allowing things to be easy.

List your favourite ways to struggle, and give them up.

46

Verdict: innocent

Have you ever felt guilty for no apparent reason, as if you were in the dock being tried for something that you never did?

The type of guilt that I'm talking about is less of an emotion and more of a way of life. It pervades everything and causes untold misery.

For example, at work you may feel like a fraud, in your relationship you may become defensive, and when relaxing you may give yourself a hard time.

Guilt is irrational and distressing. It is the result of the erroneous belief that you have done something wrong. It often stems from a childhood feeling of unworthiness. Decide now to sign a peace treaty by forgiving yourself and giving up guilt.

*Write a statement declaring
your innocence and read it often.*

47

Stop trying to impress

What do you do in order to look good? Stock your wardrobe with expensive labels? Fill your conversation with long words? Name drop until even you become uncomfortable? The list can go on and on.

Understandably, we have a great need to be accepted by others. This is very natural. The problem occurs when we begin to compromise ourselves and become inauthentic.

When we become overly concerned with the need to look good we move away from our centre. It is this centre that provides the foundation for real happiness and joy. This centre is our innate wholeness and value. We do not need to embellish it with anything in order to be acceptable.

If somebody does not see you for who you are, it says more about them than it does about you.

Commit to your authentic self —
look good naturally.

48

Be real

Several years ago The Happiness Project
brought Patch Adams to the UK. Patch is the
doctor who pioneered a 'joyful philosophy' for
medical care. A movie starring Robin Williams
has been made about his life. His was no
ordinary achievement and he is no ordinary
man.

To express his unique approach Patch dresses
as a clown. This can sometimes be a challenge.
One particular experience stands out. We were
at Dublin airport flying to Edinburgh, with
thousands of Scottish rugby fans making their
way home. I shall never forget the expressions

on their faces as they tried to assess Patch. They couldn't work him out. 'A 6-foot-6-inch man with pink hair down to his waist? In the middle of an airport?' However, Patch won them over immediately when he expressed the real person underneath all the make-up.

Being real may appear a simple equation for happiness, yet the challenge can be immense. The keys are to listen and follow your heart, to have the courage to go against popular opinion and to honour your convictions.

Develop the capacity to be honest and authentic in your life and relationships.

49

Meet your needs

As new parents the primary thing that my wife Veronica and I agreed upon was that we would meet the needs of our daughter. Since then I have witnessed that if her needs are met she is happy, and if they're not, she let's us know!

Adults are no different. Think about how you are when your needs are met. You function well. Everything is working. When they are not, trouble brews.

Ask yourself, 'Where are my needs not being met in my work, relationships and life?' For instance, maybe you need more recognition in your work. Perhaps you need to be listened to more in your relationships. Maybe you need to have more fun. Once you have identified these needs, be willing to have them met.

Be prepared to ask your colleagues and friends for the support you need in order to give yourself the chance to be truly fulfilled.

Needs are natural, so respect them.

50

Re-evaluate expectations

Whenever we pick up a magazine or paper we
see celebrities presented as role models. This
can have a powerful effect on our expectations
of what we 'should' be able to achieve.
Advertising bolsters this image of unattainable
happiness.

I addressed this dilemma when I was speaking
at a dinner. It was a wealthy audience and I
was intrigued by their response to my

questions. The majority revealed that a primary cause of unhappiness for them was carrying too high expectations. In my work with clients dealing with unfulfilled expectations, we begin to challenge the validity of each expectation and where it comes from. This process enables us to re-evaluate what's truly meaningful and what is artificial.

Ask yourself, 'Do my expectations support me or undermine me?' Your re-evaluation will provide you with a new sense of what's possible.

**Let go of expectations
and let happiness in.**

51

Stop waiting
– start living

What are you waiting for? Enough money?
Your perfect body weight? The right job? Your
ideal partner? At The Happiness Project we
refer to this condition as the WAIT Problem,
i.e. waiting for all the jigsaw pieces of your life
to come together before you can be happy.

Deciding to give up the WAIT Problem and committing to happiness could be your turning point. When you start living now, you put yourself firmly back in the driving seat. Ask yourself, 'What am I waiting for?' Then, 'What am I really waiting for?' Having identified the real issues, let them go.

All sorts of doors will open as you free yourself from this self-imposed limitation.

No amount of waiting will guarantee you happiness.

52

No judgement, know happiness

Self-judgement is like a dark cloud hanging over us, smothering our creative expression and spontaneous joy. It leaves us with a tainted impression of ourselves and prevents us from fulfilling our true potential.

The trouble with self-judgement is that it can never offer a solution, only a series of self-condemnations. Its roots lie in fear. Self-judgement is a million miles away from constructive criticism.

You can tell self-judgement by its tone of voice. 'What's wrong with you?' 'You never get it right.' 'You are such a failure.' 'You haven't got a clue.'

The next time you find you're judging yourself, stop and forgive yourself. Be willing to replace self-judgement with self-acceptance.

Commit to self-acceptance one day at a time.

53

No more sacrifice

Several years ago my wife Veronica and I discussed what we enjoyed doing in life. Near to the top of my list was playing tennis and she suggested that I join a club. I argued against it, saying that it was 'too much of a luxury, too time-intensive and too much fun!' Afterwards I recognised what a sacrifice I was making by not joining.

I signed up.

Where are you in sacrifice? Do you play the role of martyr at work, in relationships or with your health? If so, it's time to give it up. Be willing to be self-generous rather than self-sacrificing. You're worth it.

When you stop playing your sacrifice record over and over again, you will find that you have so much more to offer. Sociable, creative, optimistic, generous and kind – you will be all of this.

Giving to yourself means
you have more to give to others.

54

Be curious

Watching my daughter India play, I see how her curiosity about the everyday objects that I have taken for granted creates a world of wonder and excitement.

Inventors are also great examples of people who regard the world with inquisitive eyes, constantly considering new ideas and possibilities. For example, James Dyson, the creator of the first bag-free vacuum cleaner, is someone with an amazing ability to turn his questioning mind into a phenomenal business opportunity.

Ask yourself, 'What is fascinating about myself and my life?' Then simply wonder at the miracle of being alive.

Make a point of getting curious about one thing each day.

55

Smile at your inner dialogue

One morning I woke up feeling tense. Nothing had happened, but I was restless. It was not an uncommon occurrence so I decided to really confront the issue. I had a meeting to attend and was faced with an hour alone in the car. As I set off I tried to talk myself out of the tension. It didn't work. Then I experienced a transformation.

I decided to let the tension talk to me. I imagined it as a separate voice. I gave it permission to talk and for the next half hour

I listened to what it wanted to say. It told me things such as, 'You're not good enough. What's wrong with you? You're not doing enough.' As it continued, I realised that it was the voice of self-judgement. This recognition enabled me to see it as an old friend. As it came to its own natural conclusion, I felt relaxed and centred again.

We all have an inner dialogue. Make sure that you give it space and don't take it personally. Your willingness to befriend it will diminish its influence.

What you listen to can be transformed.

56

Breathe easy

At the heart of every spiritual practice is the breath. It's what connects us with our life force, and yet for something so significant we tend to miss out on harnessing its potential.

It's easy in our busy lives to become unaware of how we breathe, but breathing has a very significant effect on how we function. When stressed, we breathe in a shallow, rapid way which compounds the feeling of tension. On the other hand, when we're happy our breath is open, full and relaxed.

Let's use this open and relaxed form of breathing to benefit our everyday life.

Begin by focusing on your breath. Place one hand on your stomach and the other on your chest. The breath should enter your stomach first. If it doesn't, focus on breathing into your stomach, making your hand rise. Start gently and then gradually breathe more deeply. This will open up your breath and eventually help it to become easy and effortless.

Start the day by taking five full and open breaths.

57

Create internal sunshine

On my happiness workshops I ask participants what they associate with happiness. One of the most common replies is sunshine. This is always followed by a laugh because to live in the UK and rely on the sun for happiness is not a wise move! However, the ability to generate your own internal warmth is a valuable tool.

If you believe that a sense of relaxation, the draining away of tension, more energy and a brighter mood are all connected with sunshine, then you'd be right. But we need to learn to create these states with or without sunshine.

The technique of visualisation can be a great help. The benefit of using mental imagery is that you react as if you actually were in the situation you create. Take some time out and see if the following visualisation works for you.

Sit comfortably. Close your eyes and take some deep breaths. Picture a big, silver movie screen in your mind. Project the image of a favourite beach onto the screen. See the deep blue sea, hear the waves, feel the warmth of the sun on your skin. Notice what you're wearing, the relaxed way you're lying and the calm smile on your face. Freeze the frame. Sink into the image. Enjoy.

Picture the sun shining in your mind whenever you need a boost.

58

Health matters

Another thing that participants on my happiness workshops associate with happiness is health. However, I have met remarkably inspiring people with terminal illnesses who glow with happiness. It is always a powerful reminder for me that real happiness is not dependent on our physical state. Though I have no doubt that it's harder to experience happiness when you have a health problem, I believe that illness can be a great teacher providing valuable lessons.

Certainly I have learnt to listen to my body whenever I am under the weather. Understanding what it's telling me and realising what I have ignored (to my detriment) leads to a rebalancing of myself.

Do you make your health a priority? Are you looking after yourself well? If not, decide to change your habits. Check the basics such as nutrition, exercise and sleep patterns to ensure that you are getting the right balance. Taking care of your health is a component of happiness.

Listen to your body,
it's telling you something.

59

Schedule space

Do you find yourself so busy, rushed and living on the edge that even reading this page feels like a guilty sin?

Crazy schedules mean that time has become the most valuable resource today. We're living in a cash-rich, time-poor economy, where people would rather spend money than time.

Imagine doing absolutely nothing.

I mean it. Five minutes every day where you
stop.

Schedule this space into your diary right now.

Space to breathe. Space to be. Space to listen.

Space to feel. Space to reflect.

Do you find yourself feeling better already?
It's surprising just how quickly this works.

Each moment of space
is an invitation for happiness.

Have courage

'How are you?' Our replies come thick and
fast. 'Not so bad', 'Not too bad', 'Not bad'. At
The Happiness Project we call this condition
'Not-so-badderitis!

Other responses along the same lines include,
'Can't complain', 'Mustn't grumble',
'Soldiering on', 'Surviving', 'Bearing up' and
'Keeping my head above water'.

It's inspired stuff.

What if you did respond with, 'Happy', 'Thriving', 'Well' or 'Great'? The probability is that it would be met with disbelief.

There is no doubt about it, being publicly happy is a courageous act. You may feel as if you're going against the tide. Yet it's essential to have the courage to stand up for your happiness.

Ask yourself, 'How prepared am I to declare my happiness?' Your willingness to share it will reap generous rewards.

If you're happy, share it.

61

Rewrite your life story

Look back over your life and ask yourself how you interpret what has happened. Do you regard yours as a blessed existence or as a series of unfortunate and painful experiences? Whatever your interpretation is, I wonder if you can see that it's created purely by the way you have chosen to see your life?

This may be difficult for you to accept, but as you reflect upon your reactions to the important events in your life, you will see that they have shaped your reality. This is what we call 'the story of your life'.

So how would you describe your 'story' so far? Has it been an inspiration or a drama? A comedy or a tragedy? A love story or a tale of heartbreak?

We all have a 'story' to tell. Once you recognise that you're the author of your life script, then you can begin to rewrite it. For instance, if your 'story' has been one of loss and pain, betrayal, hurt and rejection, your willingness to let go of your interpretation will open new doors for you.

Be prepared to rewrite your life 'story' in order to enjoy happiness now.

Become a bestseller with your life story.

62

There's always a way through

Feeling stressed? Tired? Frustrated? Good, because it means that you are ready to change your life for the better.

People are often confused when they tell me their difficulties and I respond with a positive declaration. However, confusion is valuable because it shows that some questioning is taking place. It's only too easy to slip into a state of resignation when times are tough rather than seeing that you have options.

For example, when your shoulders are up level with your ears, your brain is knocking on your head and your nervous system is auditioning for a part in *High Anxiety*, it is a clear message that there is a better way of managing your life.

When you reach an apparent dead-end, tell yourself that there must be a better way. Your willingness to embrace something new will open you to new solutions.

Problems are opportunities
waiting to be seen.

63

Give up grievances

'My boss doesn't appreciate me.' 'My partner is selfish and lazy.' 'I always have to call to keep in touch with friends.' 'Everything is too expensive.' 'Life is just not fair.' Does this list sound familiar?

The trouble with having grievances is that you suffer as a result. Your immune system can be seriously weakened by holding on to all of the above.

Ask yourself, 'What grievances do I have that damage my happiness?'

Once you have identified them, be prepared to let them go, each and every one. Your willingness to move on will pay dividends.

Be prepared to see life differently.

64

Live wisely

At the heart of Buddhist teachings is the eternal question, 'Did you learn to live well?' I think it is important to reflect upon this question as often as possible. It encourages a clear definition of what living well actually means to you and provides guidance for the way ahead.

In the past I defined living well as earning x amount of money, ticking off my 'to do' list, winning at tennis and attracting new girlfriends. No wonder happiness eluded me!

Take a moment, close your eyes, place your attention on your heart and say to yourself, 'What living well means to me is...' Don't edit your answer. Simply notice the message you receive and commit to living it. Living well requires you to listen to your 'inner-tuition', which is the voice of your soul.

Living well promotes happiness.

65

No limits

Imagine happiness delivered to you so tightly wrapped in a box that there is no way that it can get out! Jammed and stuck, your happiness eludes you. Try as you might, you cannot get the box open. It's impossible.

If you experience happiness as being in short supply, you probably need to discover where you are blocking it, because the truth is that happiness is unlimited.

Say to yourself, 'The ways I limit happiness are...' and register your answers. Common responses include: 'Too much happiness is dangerous' and 'People will think I've lost the plot'. Be willing to travel 180 degrees in your mind. See a picture of unlimited happiness and rejoice in the opportunities it brings.

Let happiness out of the box
and watch the glow spread.

66

Give your heart fully

I presented a powerful transformational
seminar recently for a large corporation. In the
introductions I asked people to reveal their
most prized possession and their greatest
success. When it arrived at my turn I surprised
myself by saying that for me my daughter
India fulfilled both criteria.

This was a big change for me. In the past my answers would have been linked to my work. I realised that I had given my heart so fully to India that she had given a whole new meaning to my life.

It is not important what you give you heart to, but give it. Whether it's a small child, a partner, a project, a home or a garden, you are fully engaged in the creative process of living.

Give wholeheartedly to what you love.

67

Choose the best – forget the rest

We live in a world of multiple choice. We're bombarded with choices, whether it's which product to buy, which book to read, which channel to watch, which food to eat. McDonald's promotes a McChoice menu consisting of 40,415 choices. Imagine eating a different combination of the same food each day for the next 110 years!

We're ruled by convenience and the easy choice. Everything is available now. But the truth is that when it comes to making discerning choices, they involve time, patience and dedication.

Happiness requires this commitment.

Become more focused on those choices that really support your happiness and drop those that don't.

At the beginning of each day ask yourself, 'What choice supports my happiness today?'

68

Be your own guru

I was aged twenty-four and attending a personal development programme in America. I was searching for more answers. I wanted more wisdom. I shared with the group my belief that I would be wise by the time I reached forty. Until then I would have to suffer the frustration of unknowing.

Everybody laughed! The majority of the group were already over forty and still searching, and nobody felt particularly wise. The trainer responded by suggesting that rather than searching for answers, I should start listening to the wisdom that lies within.

Thus begun a journey of listening and acting on my inner voice of wisdom.

Do you regard yourself as a wise person? Or do you see wisdom as something unattainable? Say to yourself right now, 'I am a wise person.' How does it feel? Your willingness to embrace your inner wisdom will begin a new dialogue that will sustain you throughout your life.

Listen to and act on your inner wisdom.

Don't give up

In moments of difficulty do you give up on believing in happiness? When your relationship has hit the rocks, work is too much and your self-worth seems to have disappeared, it's only too easy to lose yourself in a sense of cynicism and resignation.

Mild misery, quiet desperation and noble martyrdom are often familiar friends at times like this. Especially playing the noble martyr card. I should know. I have played it enough before. 'Poor me.' 'My life is so hard.' 'Nobody understands.' This victim role does not help anyone. In fact, it's the greatest block to seeing the potential in any situation.

It's often at those moments when we're tempted to opt out that we're closest to a breakthrough.

A key to a greater sense of happiness can be just around the corner. Be prepared to give up your resignation and make yourself available to happiness again. New solutions will emerge that you might not even have considered.

Keep faith with happiness.

We're all in the same boat

How often in your everyday life do you find yourself focusing on the differences between you and the people around you? Whether it be their colour, cultural background, faith or work, each time you focus on a difference you create a sense of separation, which is a block to happiness.

Recognising that we are human beings consisting of the same human mind, body and emotions is a validating experience.

We all originate from the same source.
This awareness of our essential nature allows
us to connect with others more easily. It gives
rise to a more fulfilling and rewarding
communication.

Recognising our connection also enables us to
have a greater sense of belonging and meaning
in our lives.

Let go of seeing differences
and experience a greater sense of joy.

71

Be open to relationship gifts

It never ceases to amaze me how from one moment to the next relationships can fill our lives with both wonderful gifts and enough material for an entire soap opera! This is the dance that takes place in relationships – one between receiving so much and acting out so much.

We often believe that what lie between ourselves and happiness are the relationship conflicts we experience. However, this is an illusion. The truth is that if somebody is in your life there is a gift for you to give and to receive. These gifts are enormous, consisting of such things as love, friendship, honesty, support, thoughtfulness, generosity, humour and fun.

The next time you find yourself in a power struggle, feeling jealousy or resentment towards somebody, ask your higher mind, 'What is the gift to be revealed from in relationship?' In the intensity of the drama it can be hard to see the underlying gift, but it is always there.

You are a gift-bearer and a gift-receiver
in every relationship.

72

End comparisons

One of the quickest routes to unhappiness is comparing yourself with others.

We all do it. It's a social condition. We've learnt to do it as a way of measuring our worth.

Who do you compare yourself with? Is it your partner, a work colleague, a celebrity (someone you have never even met!)?

The truth is that you'll come out feeling better about yourself or worse. You'll see yourself as

more talented, more attractive and more
successful, or the opposite. Either way, this isn't
going to give you real happiness; it's a
temporary fix.

Being stuck in comparison disempowers you.
It cuts you off from accepting yourself as who
you are and prevents you from expressing
this fully.

Learn to value your uniqueness. Your
willingness to give up comparison will enable
you to move forwards based on your truth.

Focus on your uniqueness.

73

Overcome adversity

As I was sitting down to write this chapter I received a phone call from our neighbour. She was in a state of shock because she'd just found out that the managing agents of our building had gone bankrupt. In the middle of major building works. With our money in their bank account. And just before my family and I were about to go off on holiday.

This was a moment to practise what I preach! I was tempted to fly into a rage and track the

agent down. Instead I decided to call upon the
help of my friends, get advice and handle it
one step at a time.

There are times in our lives when we are faced
with major obstacles and sometimes it's hard
to respond constructively. However, we do have
the ability to rise to challenges in ways that can
strengthen our lives for the better.

The next time you experience one of life's
hiccups, use it for your own growth. Problems
occur every day. We cannot control them but
we can decide whether they will control us.

Within adversity there is a gift.

74

Let go

Have you ever watched a fly trying to escape through a window? The manic buzzing noise tells the fly's story – 'try harder'! It's a sorry sight, as only a few feet away there is an opening to freedom. If only the fly had the wisdom to let go of its futile attempts at escape and head in the right direction!

How often do you find yourself holding on to a game plan that has clearly had its day? We are creatures of habit and can find it hard to let go of past unhelpful behaviours such as stubbornness and struggle.

We can fall into the trap of doing the same thing over and over again, while hoping for a different result. Much like the fly.

Ask yourself, 'What does it cost me to hold on to my unhelpful habits?' Does it cost you your happiness, your sense of vitality, your joy? Clarifying the price that you pay will help you to let go.

Once you have started, an open door awaits you.

Your willingness is the key to letting go.

75

Get balanced

On a scale of 0–10 how much time, energy and attention do you give to the following areas?

Work

Relationships

Self

Spirituality

Health

Leisure

Do they score around the same amount, or is there an imbalance?

The ability to balance our priorities on a day-to-day level is good for happiness. It gives us a sense of control over our destiny and helps us to feel optimistic.

When we're out of balance we lose perspective on life, and this can result in stress, relationships breaking down and work problems appearing unmanageable.

Ask yourself, 'What's the first step I can take to regain balance?' Go back to the initial list and decide what you need to put more energy into. Your willingness to act will have an immediate effect on your wellbeing.

Balance helps you to
rediscover your happiness.

76

Resolve the work ethic

Have you noticed how the working week has got longer and longer? In fact British people now work longer hours than people in any other European country – and the funny thing is that we appear to be proud of it. We even wear our work ethic as a badge of honour! We seem to have taken it to the extreme, and we're suffering as a result.

Ask yourself, 'Do I put my work before my family and friends? Is it interfering with my home life?' If so, be willing to read on.

Obviously, work is great. It's important for our sense of self-worth, belonging and financial security, but not at the expense of our relationships, family, health and, ultimately, happiness. If you find that your life is simply spent recovering from work, it's time to achieve a new balance, a new beginning.

Aim to work smarter not harder
in order to be happy.

77

More is an illusion

Have you ever felt like a hamster on a wheel pedalling furiously trying to create 'more'? More money, more success, more power, more love. Yet more is never enough.

I would like you to consider that more can never be enough – until you understand that who you are is enough.

This need for 'more' is primarily driven by a sense of lack and fear. We tell ourselves, 'Who

I am isn't enough', 'What I have isn't enough.'
These voices remove us from our wholeness
and our sense of self-worth.

Imagine what your life would look and feel
like without this underlying fear. It would be
an abundant place, free from the constant
addiction to more.

Now is the time to come home to your true
self, to reconnect with the essential self-worth
that is at the core of your happiness. You will
be truly thankful.

Less fear equals more happiness.

78

One-stop happiness

How many thoughts stand between you and happiness? Most people feel that happiness is far away, but the truth is that it's a much shorter journey than you might think.

Consider this idea. You are only one thought away from happiness. How does this make you feel? For many of my clients it has made happiness far more tangible and available in their lives.

Ask yourself, 'What thought stands between me and happiness?' Once you have identified it, be willing to let it go. Doing this on a regular basis keeps your mind clear of limiting thoughts that may block happiness.

The journey to happiness
is shorter than you think.

79

Your
happiness
is a gift

When my football team wins, I want to rejoice
with everyone. When it loses, I want to hide.
When I witness a breathtaking sunset, I want
to share it. When it's cold and wet, I don't
advertise it. When I hear beautiful music,
I want others to enjoy it. When it's a poor
performance, I keep quiet.

There is a natural impulse to want to share happiness. On many occasions I have witnessed people deriving the greatest happiness from offering the gift of happiness to others. Life becomes meaningless very quickly once we stop sharing the gifts available to us. Happiness has no limits, so the more you give, the more you receive.

Be generous with your happiness,
because the more you give,
the more you get.

Receive well

How would you respond if somebody offered you happiness on a plate? No strings attached, no conditions to meet and no guilt required. It seems almost too good to be true.

Ask yourself, 'Would I receive happiness easily or, knowing myself as I do, would I feel uncomfortable and reject it?'

We are all faced with this possibility every day. Happiness is available to us here and now. The big question is, are we willing to receive it?

Be willing to release your struggle and
resistance in order to let the wisdom of
happiness pervade. The truth is you don't have
to do anything. Self-acceptance and your own
innate worthiness are at the heart of receiving
happiness.

**Your willingness to receive
is a wonderful gift.**

81

You're OK

On average, by the age of eighteen we will have been praised and encouraged 30,000 times — and most of this praise and encouragement we will have received by the time we are three. By contrast, we will have been criticised and discouraged over 250,000 times. It comes as no surprise therefore that for the countless clients I have worked with there is one dominant belief that causes more damage than any other — the belief that we're not good enough. This self-limiting belief plays havoc with our perception and causes us untold misery. Characteristics of 'I'm not good enough' syndrome include:

- Striving for perfection but never arriving.

- Undermining yourself in relationships and/or jobs.
- Not meeting your needs because they're not important enough.
- Not speaking up because what you've got to say isn't interesting enough.
- Constantly trying to prove your self-worth.

Happiness will always be out of your reach until you change your mind about yourself. Be willing to see yourself differently. You are OK. Accept this. What have you got to lose? Only your unhappiness.

Never miss an opportunity to encourage and praise yourself.

82

Choose to be lucky

Are you the type of person that buys a lottery
ticket but then doesn't check to see if you've
won? Or do you choose not to play because
you know that the odds are so high that you
will never win?

The English Oxford Dictionary defines happiness as
'fortune' and 'luck'. According to this
definition, if you don't happen to get a
winning ticket you are doomed to a life of
unhappiness.

Take a moment to consider the idea that you can choose to be lucky. While you are focusing on this I'll give you an example of a friend of mine – an incredibly 'lucky' friend. Kate has had more holidays than anyone else I know. Why? Because she believes she is lucky and with that power of belief behind her has entered every holiday competition that she can. She has won virtually all of them.

Choosing luck may mean that you live your life feeling that the world is on your side. And if you do decide to buy a ticket, you never know what might happen!

Choose luck and play the game.

83

Live your life on purpose

I travelled the world looking for my purpose.
I thought that I'd find it in America, India
definitely, Europe quite possibly, and New
Zealand was a long shot. I didn't. In fact I had
my greatest breakthrough back in London
while walking in a park!

While turning over in my mind the question
of finding my purpose, I came to the
realisation that it was something I could
choose. That I could define it for myself.
Having always believed that my purpose was
something that I would eventually find, it

came as a great relief to recognise that I could choose it instead.

I chose love. Simple as it may seem, love is the inspiration of my life. It is the bedrock for all my decision-making.

Have you felt lost or blocked in trying to find your purpose? Ask yourself, 'What purpose do I choose for my life?' Listen to your answer. Does it inspire you? Does it fill you with hope? Does it give you a sense of meaning and direction? If so, then you're on the right track.

Your inspiration is the gateway to your purpose.

84

Stop scoring own goals

Have you ever found yourself accomplishing a goal, only to find that you feel empty and deflated?

I remember the feelings of anticlimax and disillusionment that set in following the publication of my first book and moving into my first home. I should have been so happy. What was wrong? I realised in retrospect that I had placed so much emphasis on the outcome that I had missed out on enjoying the process.

Maybe now is the time to look at what you're investing your time and energy in. What are the goals that you have set yourself? Is your focus so connected to the horizon that you fail to see the landscape in front of you? If so, a change is in order.

Life is made up of a series of moments, not ultimate goals. Decide to make each moment precious. Your willingness to experience each moment as something valuable and unique will have extraordinary results.

Let your goals include all the moments along the way.

85

Live fully

Are you making the most of your life? I have
had moments when I've caught myself trying
to hold on to my life, as if I could save it for a
rainy day. This is not a good strategy for
happiness. In fact one of the biggest causes of
unhappiness is postponed happiness. We delay
it by telling ourselves that today is not a day to
be happy. Remember: happiness needs no
reason. It waits on your invitation. You can
decide to live fully by taking the lid off
happiness.

The art of living fully is about being in the moment. We tend to live so many years ahead of each day that we fail to maximise each precious instant that is available here and now. A useful tip is to ask yourself, on a scale of 0–10, how fully you are living. If you're not at level 10, discover what needs to happen to get you there. Then commit to it and watch your life flourish.

As the saying goes, life is not a dress rehearsal. Make the most of it — now.

86

Think creatively

Most of us only use an estimated three per cent of our brain power. Think about the untapped potential in your mind. It's mind-boggling!

Through our educational system we have been trained to think rationally and to block our creative thinking. Yet there is a whole other reality available to us once we embrace creative thought – a world filled with infinite possibility and opportunity that is the result of our willingness to open our minds.

Take a moment now to remember what it was like to let your mind wander as a child, to let yourself dream up extraordinary possibilities. Recognise that this capacity still lies within you.

The way to tap into your creative thinking is to simply focus on it regularly. Ask yourself, 'What creative thought would inspire me today?' Let your mind present you with answers that take you into new pastures.

Creative thinking is a talent
that lies within you —
let it out to inspire your life.

87

Take a leap

When my wife Veronica said that she wanted to have a child, I freaked! Fearing that I was already too busy and unable to handle the responsibility and expense, I had a lot of soul-searching to do.

It didn't take me too long, however, to realise what was really important to me. There wasn't any 'right' time to have a child and what it called for was a leap of faith. Thank God I did it! Of course, now I couldn't imagine life without India.

There is a saying, 'Leap and the net appears.'
Wouldn't it be nice if the net appeared first?
But life doesn't work like that. We have to take
the step off the edge and hold our nerve. It is
the only way to grow.

Ask yourself, 'What is the leap I am being
asked to take right now?' Remember there isn't
a 'right' time – just take it now.

*Every time you leap, your life
moves forward in ways you could not
even have imagined.*

88

Connect with spirit

When I was sixteen, my mother took me to an introductory talk on meditation. I remember being absolutely fascinated as I listened to everyday people talking about completely new worlds. Being introduced to different states of consciousness and the practice of meditation was the beginning of a lifelong journey into the realm of spirituality.

Nowadays my daily life includes meditation, prayer and consciously connecting with spirit. It is clear to me that when I do consciously connect, then my life works, and when I disconnect, I experience struggle and fear.

What do you do in your life that connects you with spirit? Maybe it's being in nature, listening to music, looking at beautiful art or sitting in silence. Whatever it is, make sure that you give yourself a healthy dose every week.

Before you jump into your day,
stop and connect with spirit.

89

Build up your trust fund

We live in an unpredictable world. Uncertainty is the only guarantee we have. Change is everywhere. What can we do? Trust.

Trust is the force that takes us past fear. Trust is the power that rebuilds our broken dreams. Trust is the foundation upon which our relationships can flourish. Trust is the basis for creating new levels of success. The way to build trust is to recognise how much of it we already have in our lives. Every time we sleep we trust that we'll wake up. Every time we cross the road we trust that we'll get to the other side. Now extend this innate trust into areas that cause you concern, whether it is your work, money issues or relationship difficulties.

If you're having trouble trusting immediately, then my suggestion is to begin by 'acting as if' you trusted. What I mean by this is that you adopt the role of somebody who trusts. How does it feel? What difference does it make? Let this experience inspire you to deepen your level of trust.

Imagine living life as if you trusted.

90

Laugh and the whole game changes

I was on my knees. Another broken night of sleep with our baby and it felt as if I had ants crawling in my body. Veronica was even more exhausted than me, and we wondered how we were going to get through the day ahead. Then India started chuckling. Within moments smiles had broken out all round, which very

quickly turned into full belly laughter. We had
tears rolling down our cheeks as the infectious
nature of laughter took over.

Sometimes laughter is a lifeline. When stress
has positioned your shoulders level with your
ears and your head feels as if it has gone fifteen
rounds in a heavyweight contest, laughter is
the best medicine. Releasing endorphins, the
body's natural painkillers, into the
bloodstream, laughter aids relaxation and
promotes a sense of wellbeing.

Be willing to see the funny side
in any situation.

91

Happiness and creativity go hand in hand

When I was growing up as a musician I wondered if I had to suffer great pain in order to express great creativity. My days were filled with playing the music of geniuses such as Beethoven, Mozart and Schubert, all of whom suffered greatly in their lives. Did I have to go down the same path in order to express myself?

Thankfully there was a small voice within me that believed creativity could be inspired by happiness, not just by pain. Suffering didn't have to be the prerequisite.

Nowadays I still stand by my original belief and see that happiness and creativity have a symbiotic relationship. They feed each other, they inspire each other, and this wonderful mixture creates extraordinary possibilities for our lives.

Ask yourself, 'What would I create if I let happiness inspire me?' Then let it unfold.

Commit to letting happiness inspire your creativity.

92

Everyday kindness

This is a true story. A friend of mine was walking down a busy high street. He had stopped to buy some flowers when he saw an old lady standing on her own in her front garden. Thinking to himself, 'Wouldn't it be nice if I gave her the flowers?', though aware that she might think him mad, he decided to risk it. The woman was so gratified that tears filled her eyes. She explained that nobody had given her flowers for years.

This could happen every day – small acts of kindness making a big difference.

Kindness is a powerful medicine. It restores hope, inspires love and encourages happiness. It is an indication of your strength. It is a true gift.

Make somebody's day through your willingness to be kind. Give a sincere compliment, a small gift or a genuine thank you and touch people in ways that you may not even begin to understand.

Never miss an opportunity to be kind.

93

Value compassion

While travelling to the Dalai Lama's settlement
in the foothills of the Himalayas, I had the
good fortune to meet a Canadian Buddhist
monk. It was one of those great conversations,
set against a backdrop of mad Indian driving,
about the differences between Eastern and
Western values. He had let go of his old life in
Toronto in order to become a monk and had
renounced his Western value system.

I was intrigued by him. He was doing
something that had always appealed to me.
I wanted to know more. I asked him what the

main difference was that he had experienced
between the two cultures. His reply has stayed
with me ever since: those in the East tend to
value compassion more than those in the West.
In fact it is often the path they choose to walk
in life.

At the heart of compassion is unconditional
love. It melts away judgement, creates
understanding and bridges differences. It is
also a very real demonstration of empathy.
Ask yourself, 'How can I extend compassion
today?' and act upon the answer you receive.

Put compassion at
the heart of your life.

94

Believe in yourself

I always dreamt of writing a book. There was one small stumbling block. I didn't believe that I could do it! I distinctly remember the mixture of fear and anticipation when I got my first contract. What to do? Though completing the book was a great effort, the boost to my sense of self-worth and self-belief was extraordinary. I'd had to compete with a doubting voice ringing in my head, telling me that I couldn't do it, but I had proved it wrong!

How much do you believe in yourself? It will probably fluctuate depending on the situation. For instance, you may feel confident in your work but less so in relationships. However, developing your sense of self-belief in all situations is crucial. Confidence enables you to relax. It helps you simply to be yourself, which is the gateway to happiness and fulfilment.

Ask yourself, 'What is my next step towards having greater self-belief?' Then be prepared to take a quantum leap forward.

**Believing in yourself will
conquer your self-doubt.**

95

Remember, you make a difference

The Body Shop once had a slogan that read, 'If you think you're too small to make a difference, read up on mosquitoes.' I would also like to add that, as any new parent knows only too well, it's not just small mosquitoes that can make a difference!

Who you are has an impact. You can make either a worthwhile contribution to the society around you or a detrimental one. It's up to you. Take a moment to think about the difference

you could make, if you're not already making it.
Reflect upon the contribution you make at home,
with your family and friends and through your
work, whether it is paid employment or in a
voluntary capacity. Think about the variety of
things you can do to make a difference. Maybe
you could call your mum more often, spend
more time with your kids, become a better
listener, exercise more patience, become a more
supportive neighbour.

Commit to making a valuable contribution to
your family and community.

Be imaginative.
It can be fun to make a difference.

Relax, relax, relax

A friend of mine was on holiday recently when, in the middle of nowhere, his scooter stopped working. Usually when things go wrong he gets pretty frenzied. However, this time he decided to have a swim and sort out the problem later. When he returned, he found that the scooter was just low on petrol.

Isn't it amazing how when we relax everything seems to fall into place? Yet often we only allow ourselves to relax on a Friday night or when we feel that we deserve it. But there is another way.

You can make relaxation an everyday choice.
Decide to relax before your day starts, when
you're stuck in traffic, when you're facing
another work problem.

Actively relaxing helps us to breathe more
easily and restores our sanity. It is not
dependent on how well we perform at work,
how much money we have in the bank or how
well our relationship is going.

Decide now to let relaxation become a way of
life rather than a reward you give yourself at
the end of another hard day.

Make relaxation a choice for happiness.

97

Live your values

Take a moment and point to where you think north lies. Are you sure that is the right direction? I'm going to have to take your word for it, but you might want to get a compass to double-check. There. Were you going the right way?

In this exercise north symbolises the direction that you're heading and the compass represents the core values that guide you. If you find that you're not going in the direction that you want it's a fair indication that you're

not clear about your core values. Your compass
has been giving you faulty information.

Imagine if you will that your name appears in
the dictionary followed by three adjectives that
describe you. What would they be? Ask
yourself, 'What do I stand for? What am I most
passionate about?'

When you're clear about what things are most
important to you, make sure they are placed at
the centre of your world. These are your core
values. This is your compass.

Happiness means being in touch
with your values.

98

Friendship is everything

When I first met my wife Veronica, she was living in Tokyo. As I was living in London, our relationship began with very expensive long-distance phone calls. There was a gift to this, though, as it allowed our friendship to evolve before anything else. Our friendship remains at the very heart of our relationship and sustains us through all our ups and downs.

Imagine a life without friendship. No one to share your joys and fears with. No one to offer you support and encouragement. No one to look out for you. No one to celebrate your successes with. Yet it's easy to put friendship lower down our list of priorities as we get on with our busy lives.

If you see that you're too busy to have real friendships, you're too busy!

Begin to make friendship a priority again. Be willing to invest the time, energy and attention in nurturing the relationships closest to you.

Reflect upon who is most important
to you and let them know.

99

Serve and be happy

Over the years I have become intimately acquainted with a hotel near Junction 4 of the M4 motorway. It is where I meet with my colleague Robert Holden. Consequently we have come to know a lady called Pam, who works in the hotel. Pam is a champion of service. Each time we arrive she greets us with a heart-warming smile. She takes a genuine interest in what we do and shares her latest findings from what she's read and seen on TV. Pam treats everyone in the same way. Service is not a technique that she employs. It's who she is.

What do you associate with service? Long hours and sacrifice? If so, this is a big misunderstanding. Real service is about sharing your heart and soul with others and creating trusting relationships. It involves finding out and meeting the needs of your partner, friends, family, colleagues and customers. It is a philosophy that embraces giving as the means to happiness.

Ask yourself, 'How can I serve fully each day?' Then be willing to give selflessly. You will be well rewarded for it.

Focus on what you can give,
not on what you can get.

100

Love, love, love

Stop for a moment and ask yourself what is the most important thing in your life? Is it your bank balance, your home, your job, your status? Is it your family or friends? Although these factors are obviously important components of your life, I believe that the most important thing of all is love.

The type of love that I refer to is not just an emotion; it is a philosophy for living. This approach puts love first, before everything. It is choosing to embrace life with compassion and understanding and to extend acceptance to yourself and others.

Remember, the only place that you will find happiness before love is in the dictionary! Put love first and happiness will follow.

Consciously dedicate your relationships, work and life to love.

Conclusion

Congratulations! You've made it! You have shown your commitment to happiness.

I hope that through the challenges posed on each page of this book you have come to know more about your real self and the gifts that you have to offer. Be willing to share what you've learnt. Be willing to unwrap your precious gifts. Your family, friends and colleagues will benefit. Strangers will benefit. And you will benefit in ways that you may not even be able to imagine – yet.

About the Author

Ben Renshaw is an inspirational speaker, seminar leader, success coach and broadcaster. He travels the world coaching leaders in business, health and education. He also gives public talks and workshops through The Happiness Project and The Coaching Success Partnership.

Also by Ben Renshaw:

The Secrets: 100 Ways to Have a Great Relationship

Successful But Something Missing

Together But Something Missing

Further Information

For further information about public workshops, corporate coaching and seminars, books and tapes, please contact:

The Happiness Project

Elms Court, Chapel Way, Oxford OX2 9LP

Tel: 01865 244414, Fax: 01865 248825

Email: hello@happiness.co.uk

Website: www.happiness.co.uk

The Secrets of Happiness Library

Carlson, Richard, *Don't Sweat the Small Stuff!*, Hodder & Stoughton, 1997

Greive, Bradley Trevor, *The Blue Day Book*, Robson Books, 2000

Holden, Miranda, *Boundless Love*, Rider, 2002

Holden, Robert, *Happiness NOW!*, Hodder & Stoughton, 1998

Holden, Robert, *Hello Happiness*, Hodder & Stoughton, 1999

Holden, Robert, *Shift Happens!*, Hodder & Stoughton, 2000

Holden, Robert, *Stress Busters*, HarperCollins, 1992

Holden, Robert & Renshaw, Ben, *Balancing Work and Life*, DK, 2002

James, Oliver, *Britain On the Couch*, Century Books, 1997

Jeffers, Susan, *Feel the Fear and Do It Anyway*, Rider, 1991

Kaufman, Barry Neil, *Happiness Is a Choice*, Ballantine Books, 1991

Myers, David, *The Pursuit of Happiness*, Avon Books, 1993

Peck, Scott, *The Road Less Travelled*, Rider, 1978

Renshaw, Ben, *Successful But Something Missing*, Vermilion, 2000

Renshaw, Ben, *Together But Something Missing*, Vermilion, 2001

Renshaw, Ben, *The Secrets — 100 ways to have a great relationship*, Vermilion, 2002

Spezzano, Chuck, *50 Ways To Let Go and Be Happy*, Hodder & Stoughton, 2001

Williams, Nick, *Unconditional Success*, Bantam Press, 2002

Williamson, Marianne, *A Return to Love*, Thorsons, 1992

Wilson, Paul, *Calm for Life*, Penguin, 2000